Self Portrait of Icarus as a Country on Fire

Self Portrait of Icarus as a Country on Fire

poems

ℬ❦

Jason Schneiderman

Red Hen Press | *Pasadena, CA*

Book design by Mark E. Cull
Book layout by Eurydice Dye

Library of Congress Cataloging-in-Publication Data

Names: Schneiderman, Jason, author.
Title: Self portrait of Icarus as a country on fire: poems / Jason
  Schneiderman.
Description: First Edition. | Pasadena, CA: Red Hen Press, 2024.
Identifiers: LCCN 2023052142 (print) | LCCN 2023052143 (ebook) | ISBN
  9781636281629 (trade paperback) | ISBN 9781636281636 (ebook)
Subjects: LCGFT: Poetry.
Classification: LCC PS3619.C4473 S45 2024 (print) | LCC PS3619.C4473
  (ebook) | DDC 811/.6—dc23/eng/20231108
LC record available at https://lccn.loc.gov/2023052142
LC ebook record available at https://lccn.loc.gov/2023052143

The National Endowment for the Arts, the Los Angeles County Arts Commission, the Ahmanson Foundation, the Dwight Stuart Youth Fund, the Max Factor Family Foundation, the Pasadena Tournament of Roses Foundation, the Pasadena Arts & Culture Commission and the City of Pasadena Cultural Affairs Division, the City of Los Angeles Department of Cultural Affairs, the Audrey & Sydney Irmas Charitable Foundation, the Meta & George Rosenberg Foundation, the Albert and Elaine Borchard Foundation, the Adams Family Foundation, Amazon Literary Partnership, the Sam Francis Foundation, and the Mara W. Breech Foundation partially support Red Hen Press.

First Edition
Published by Red Hen Press
www.redhen.org

ACKNOWLEDGMENTS

Grateful acknowledgment is made to the editors of the following publications, where many of these poems initially appeared, often in slightly different forms.

The Academy of American Poets Poem-a-Day, "Stories about Love / Wedding Poem for Ada & Lucas"; *American Poetry Review*: "Blood Libel / My Throte is Kut," "In the End You Get Everything Back (Liza Minnelli)," "Stalinism IV (Frida Kahlo)"; *The Believer*: "Blood and Soil"; *Connotations*: "A Story About Writing"; *The Hopkins Review*: "Gay Divorce (Free Radical)"; *Massachussets Review*: "Gay Divorce (10th Avenue)," "Star Dust"; *The Night Heron Barks*: "The Speaker in this Poem," "A Story About Translation," "You Can Be the You in this Poem"; *Two Horatio*: "At My Drink-Drunk-Unketty-Unkest"; *Upstreet*: "Catastrophist," "Theology"; *Virginia Quarterly Review*: "Dramaturgy," "Parable of the Dictator"; *Zocalo Public Square*: "Self Portrait of Icarus as a Country on Fire."

"Dramaturgy" was reprinted in *Best American Poetry 2023*, edited by Elaine Equi and David Lehman; "Wolves I Have Known (Found Poem)" was initially published in the anthology *I Want to Be Loved By You: Poems about Marilyn Monroe*, edited by Margo Taft Stever and Susana H. Case (Milk & Cake Press 2022).

These poems were written and arranged with the support of the Hermitage Artists Retreat and the Bethany Arts Community.

CONTENTS

III

Self Portrait of Icarus
as a Country
on Fire

IN THE END YOU GET EVERYTHING BACK (LIZA MINNELLI)

The afterlife is an infinity of custom shelving, where everything
you have ever loved has a perfect place, including things
that don't fit on shelves, like the weeping willow from
your parents' backyard, or an old boyfriend, exactly as he was
in your second year of college, or an aria you love, but without
the rest of the opera you don't particularly care for.
My favorite joke: Q: You know who dies? A: Everyone!
Because it's true. But ask any doctor and they'll say that
prolonging a life is saving a life. Ask anyone who survives
their surgeries, and they'll say yes, to keep living is to be saved.
I do think there's a statute of limitations on grief, like, certainly,
how someone died can be sad forever, but who can be sad
simply about the fact that Shakespeare, say, is dead, or Sappho,
or Judy Garland, or Rumi. There's a Twitter account called
LizaMinnelliOutlives, which put into the world a set of thoughts
I was having privately, but the Twitter account is kinder than
I had been, tweeting things like "Liza Minnelli has outlived
the National Rifle Association which has filed for bankruptcy"
and "Liza Minnelli has outlived Armie Hammer's career" to take
the sting out of the really painful ones, like "Liza Minnelli
has outlived Jessica Walter," or "Liza Minnelli has outlived
George Michael" or "Liza Minnelli has outlived Prince."
In my own afterlife, the custom shelves are full of Liza Minnellis—
Liza in *Cabaret*, Liza in *Arrested Development*, Liza singing
"Steam Heat" on *The Judy Garland Christmas Special*, Liza
on the *Muppet Show*, Liza in *Liza's at the Palace*, and because this is heaven,

Liza won't even know she's in my hall of loved objects,
just as I won't know that my fandom has been placed on her shelf
for when Liza Minnelli has outlived Jason Schneiderman,
waiting for Liza Minelli when Liza Minnelli has outlived
Liza Minnelli, which is what fame is, and what fame is not,
and if Jason Schneiderman outlives Jason Schneiderman,
and your love of this poem waits for me on one of my shelves,
and will keep me company for eternity, thank you for that.
I promise to cherish your love in that well-lit infinity of forever.
In one theory of the mind, the psyche is just a grab bag of lost objects,
our wholeness lost when we leave the womb, when we discover
our own body, and so on and so on, our wholeness lost and lost and lost,
as we find ourselves smaller and smaller, which is why heaven
is an endless, cozy warehouse, where nothing you loved is gone,
where you are whole because you get everything back, and by everything,
I mean you.

I

A STORY ABOUT WRITING

After the younger writer had refused the older writer,
it seemed to the younger writer that both the proposition
and the refusal were rather embarrassing events
not be retold, and the younger writer, with all good intentions,
decided to tell no one, particularly because the younger writer
felt curiously protective of the older writer's reputation,
and secretly, the younger writer feared that having refused
the older writer was actually a sign of prudery,
bourgeois morality, and overall non-bohemian-boringness-
and-boorishness. One night, many years later, the younger writer
became drunk and told a group of same-age-writers
about the advance of the older writer and the resulting refusal.
The younger writer, discreet in indiscretion, swore the other writers
to secrecy, but on hearing the confession, they laughed,
as almost all of them had also been propositioned
by the very same older writer, and while some had
said yes and some had said no, none of them felt
that the story had anything close to the gravity that
the younger writer felt it did. Realizing that his great secret
was in fact of no weight, the distraught younger writer
began to cry. When the same-age-writers asked about his tears,
the younger writer revealed how terrible it felt to have
carried a secret of no importance, to which his same-age-writer
friends said, *Don't cry, young writer. This story*
makes us love you more than ever.

STORIES ABOUT LOVE /
WEDDING POEM FOR ADA & LUCAS

In one story, the lovers are two halves
split by jealous gods, and in another story,

the lovers are victims of a wicked baby
with a bow and arrow. In one story,

love means never touching, but exchanging
a lot of handkerchiefs, and in another story,

love means a drastic change in brain
chemistry that lasts a year, even though

the after effects are lifelong. In one story,
love is the north star guiding sailors,

and in one story love is a sharp blade,
a body of water, and a trophy all at once.

The truth is that love is nothing but itself,
an axiomatic property of humankind,

like storytelling and explanation-giving,
which explains why everyone explains

love in stories, the way I once called it
a form of disappearing, and my favorite

philosopher called it a holiday. Listen,
storytelling animals: today, we say, love

is only love. Put down the crossbow, baby.
Put down the handkerchief, Lancelot.

Put away the easy chair, Babs. Let's let love
be felt in its touch and be known by its face.

Let's let love speak Ada and Lucas,
and then let's let love be silent.

A STORY ABOUT TRANSLATION

What he said to me was quite simple,
but I had to bring it into my language first.

"I went away from her, by my own
volition, in one direction," he said,

or was the information contained
in the choice of verb, the prefix,

the tense, the gender. "You left her,"
I said. "But you told me you weren't

together." "No," he said, "We were
together." Which was uncomplicated,

the truth straightening everything out
after so many tangled lies.

YOU CAN BE THE YOU IN THIS POEM

and no one else has to know. It can be our secret,
and you can blush when your husband asks, or not,
since the desires we share are not for each other,
but aligned in parallel, which is why we look hot
together in our bathing suits but won't have sex,
which I've never done with a girl by the way,
and is it OK that I called you a girl when we're both
at the exact midpoint between forty and fifty.
You can be the you in this poem because
you're so good at letting everyone else be the you
in your poems, at letting so many people be the you
in your life, so take a turn here, where you can not
be the speaker as long as you need to catch your breath,
and I'll brew you some coffee, put a roast in the oven,
and make us some chocolate chip cookies for dessert.
I still believe that love cuts out the bottom twenty percent
of suffering, though with diminishing returns, and that
it goes both ways, that the lover and beloved both
suffer less, if they're doing it right, and who says
romantic love gets to go to the front of the line?
At the end of this poem, we'll go back to our marriages
(mine dissolving), our cozy houses (mine leaking),
and you'll put your kids to bed, and when you
lie down exhausted at the end of the day,
you can be the you in this poem,
and you won't have to have written a thing.

THE SPEAKER IN THIS POEM

We used to make a big deal of it—how the speaker is not the author,
rolling our eyes whenever someone made such a rookie mistake,
before we poet-splained how even the so-called confessionals
aren't all that confessional, like try getting some autobiography
out of a Plath poem! (Hint: her father wasn't a statue or a Nazi
or even footwear.) It was a kind of foundational gospel, but
the distinction used to get us into all sorts of odd situations,
like the half-hour discussion I once led that kept coming back
to how the boyfriend in the poem seemed to be less into the speaker
in the poem than the speaker in the poem seemed to realize,
and the class consensus was that the speaker (in the poem)
really needed to break up with the boyfriend (in the poem),
which wasn't really a craft concern, but we all played our parts,
and it went much better than the conference where I realized
that the star-crossed lovers in a poem were only star-crossed
because the speaker in the poem was a senior in college
and the president of a sorority that would never accept her dating
a freshman (in the poem) from her sorority's corresponding
fraternity (in the poem). Again, not quite a craft concern,
and I should probably have been more open to the obstacle
as an obstacle, but come on people, a three year age gap
when everyone is past the age of consent? Just date the guy.
These days I think you're supposed to assume that the speaker
is the author, and that it would be offensive in a certain way,
to assume a voice that is not your own, even though persona
abounds, and just the other day I heard a famous poet scoff,

when asked a question after a reading, at the assumption
that everything in his poems is true. I felt bad for the questioner,
but I'm glad the famous poet stood up for persona,
because to be honest, I miss the distinction, the way it built
a little wall between me and the reader, the way the poem
could be ninety percent true, and that the ten percent imaginary
was just enough to keep me safe, the way it made me feel
like an actor, nude on stage, but lit in such a way that nothing
could be clearly seen, except in the most flattering
shadows and outlines.

THEOLOGY

The god of fire, sadly, is also the god of tattoos,
so the needle burns and the fire is indelible,
and whatever is burned, is burned into flesh.
When the god of fire could find no mate,
the god of dating apps suggested he consider
the god of water, since only water is unafraid of fire,
even though they could never touch. The god of water
is also the god of music, and every year, when she
swipes right and then left across her digital surface,
sending the god of fire her desire and regrets,
written out as sheet music, he burns her answer,
and the music is heard by him alone. What she has
composed is burned also onto her skin,
as is tradition, the water cooling the burn,
and the fish leaping up with joy. This story
is not quite true. They are bound, yes, but
theirs is not the courtship ritual their acolytes
believe it to be. Being mated is a better story,
so the two dear friends agreed long ago
to let their worshippers think of them as coupled
but uncoupled, because somewhere along the line,
the love of friends became less interesting
than the love of lovers. Every year, these gods
ask their acolytes to join them in worship,
to write on their skin, to burn their regrets
and to sing two songs. One you know.

It goes "Oh say shalom bimromav."
The other has the same tune, but the words
are, "Oh Sushi. Sushi, sushi, sushi." Which makes
everyone laugh. You can laugh too if you like.

AT MY DRINK-DRUNK-
DRUNKETTY-UNKEST

I laid down in the road to see the stars
more clearly. I laughed a tequila shot
through my nose onto a man trying
to pick me up at a club. I decided I had
to translate Akhmatova at that very moment,
and woke up my host family by searching loudly
for her collected works. I threw up
in someone's bed, again through my nose,
which may be a theme in my drunkenness.
I called my friend's green card marriage
a "green card marriage" for the entirety
of a party, despite her insistence
that her gay husband was her husband
and that her family was not a ploy
or a trick or a legal fiction. Each time I stopped
drinking so heavily, for a year, two years,
three years, and I'm not admitting
to much here: a handful of stories across
two decades, the moments I thought
I ought to drink a bit less, and yet it bears
saying that every weepy drunk considers
himself a kind drunk, every mean drunk
considers himself an honest drunk,
and every handsy drunk considers himself
a flirty drunk. And is it so terrible, the joys
and regrets of drunkenness, if they're just

a one-off, if they don't become a habit,
if we can disappear and come back?
I'm not sorry I saw the stars from
that gutter, though my sober sympathies lie
with the sober driver who was furious
that I had almost made him a murderer.
What I remember best is those stars,
and how they were as beautiful as any stars
could be and how much they meant to me
with my inhibitions stripped, and how well
I can still see them now.

CATASTROPHIST

Your heart doesn't have to break every day.
It's OK if sometimes trees are just trees,
and all the leaves on the ground look exactly
like all the other leaves you've already seen
in your life-long life. If some days,
you don't even bother to look closely
at the flowers as you keep on walking toward
wherever you were going, that's OK too.
Most of life, if you're lucky, is pretty boring,
filled with unburned houses, uncrashed cars,
unsick friends, unfled countries,
and unshot schools. The parts that hurt—
the parts where you aren't sure how you'll live
through them—those only happen in the life
you live. In your own life. I don't know
how to say this, except that you can only be hurt
in the life you've actually lived. I've spent so much time
in the hypothetical, thinking if I had just left
the house five minutes later, I wouldn't have been
in that car accident; if I had worn something

less flamboyant, they wouldn't have followed

us home; and other things, too, that I'm not ready

to talk about, may never be ready to say out loud.

I once spent three years living a hypothetical life,

living my life like someone who got on the wrong train,

and the right train was on a parallel track, so I could see

the people on the right train but not get to them,

and I lived like someone who had made a mistake

so terrible that he would never be at home in his own

life again. But no one knows what else would

have happened, except God. And maybe that's what

God is, or what makes God God—the way he's

keeping track of all the catastrophes that could have

happened but didn't. Maybe God wants you to know that

staying in last night really did save your life, but to you

it was just another Friday, and as bad as it is

for humans to live with all the terrible things

that every human has ever done, God lives

with all the other things we might have done,

or could have had done to us,

and that's why he stays silent, so we don't know

how much worse it could have been, or perhaps

how much better. Supposedly, there's an indigenous tribe

somewhere that measures all other virtues

against fear and caution. Among this people,

whoever comes up with the worst case scenario

gets to be in charge, and the children compete

over who can express the most worry and fear,

or something like that, or that was the story

they told the nice, white, visiting anthropologist,

because that was the one she wanted to hear,

or the story she seemed to like best.

When I heard the radio program about them

I thought that I would do quite well among

those people, and I couldn't quite understand

why the announcer seemed so condescending.

I've had three catastrophic thoughts today,

and none of them seem likely to come true,

and yet I have been carrying around those fears,

trying to keep them at bay, pretending I'm not

panicking over a narrative entirely in my head,

and maybe it would be nice to live among people

who admired me for my fears, instead of wanting

to reassure me of how unlikely they are to come true.

It's not easy to live just one life, and yet

we are called upon to do just that,

to live with the openness of the future

and the hurts of the past. So the more boring

each day, the better. David Foster Wallace

wrote an essay about a chicken who lives every day

without knowing that it is being raised

to the slaughter. His point is that all the data points

can suggest that your life will continue as it is,

unless you know the larger plans of the universe.

But screw you, DFW. We're not chickens.

Here's the story I tell myself when I'm afraid

of the worst coming true. I remind myself

that Marie Antoinette was queen over and over again,

every single day for years and years. She only had

her head cut off once.

STAR DUST

OK, fine, so we're all made of stars, but being made of stars
is like being descended from Noah or Adam—it's no big deal
if you truly believe it—and what good is it to me that our sweat
is made of star dust, that the unsanitary hand dryers at my school
are made of star dust in the star dust bathrooms that the nursing
department can't use because it turns out the star dryers
are just blowing the star feces on our star hands all over the place?
What good is it to me that the train to work is a star train
or that my job is a star job, or that the star human star body
contains nine to eleven star pints of star blood? When I was
star seven I was star woken, star gently, in the early morning,
because my star mother was losing her star blood. She collected
the star blood in star cartons, which had held the star milk
I drank on my star cereal, to make measurement of the blood
for the star doctors at the star hospital where she and my
star father went to complete the miscarriage of her star fetus,
while I went to the house of her star friend, quietly, sleepily,
and I didn't even miss a star day of star school. Oh stars.
Will you listen when I tell you I remember this? Stars,
it happened five times, because my star mother wanted more star life.
She wanted to be a mother more times than she succeeded,
and she only stopped so she wouldn't die, which was a relief,
because I wanted her not to die, and I think it made my mother
sad that I didn't want to make more lives as much as she had,

and I think that's what she meant when she made me promise
over and over again that I wouldn't ever hurt myself, even though
I had never shown any inclination toward self-harm or suicide,
and yet, she brought it up over and over as though she knew
something I didn't about myself, and even though I thought I knew
something about her, and her blood, and the empty milk cartons
we kept on hand for the next time she had to keep track
of the blood she was losing, maybe I was wrong. Thirty years later,
when all those fears of her bleeding to death seemed trapped
in some amber of memory, she died because her star lungs
were too wet to carry the star oxygen to her star blood.
I'm so sorry, star mother. I'm so sorry, star corpse. Be at peace,
for now, in the star ground, as I carry forward this star life,
so star wasted on star me, the life you star wanted to make
so star badly, this star life you star wanted enough to risk death for,
and here I am with no star children of my own, waiting to star crawl
into the star earth, saying I'm sorry, so sorry, thank you
for this life, star mother, so sorry, so sorry, I just don't want it,
so sorry, so sorry, I just want it to be over, so sorry.

II

SELF PORTRAIT OF ICARUS
AS A COUNTRY ON FIRE

Can we talk about the wax? The way the wax
would have felt on his skin, slick
at the first signs of melting, a spreading
warmth that felt so good he flew closer
to the sun, the sensation a full body coating
of intoxicating heat, before the wax
began to burn, to cover him like napalm,
to coat his body in something like jet fuel
and feathers, consuming him as surely
as the coat Medea prepared for Jason's bride.
I think my mother named me Jason
because she wanted me to live past the tragedies
she knew would be my lot, to keep going after
the bodies had piled up on stage, but I've always
felt like Icarus, a flaming ball of wax
and feather, not a beautiful boy falling out
of the sky, but a charred corpse, plummeting
to the ocean. I took the name Icarus
when I felt the wax begin to melt
on my skin. I'm not falling from the sky
just yet. The burn is still a spreading warmth.

DRAMATURGY

I'm writing a play about a Kommandant at Auschwitz
who recognizes one of the Jewish prisoners
as a famous poet, and as the Kommandant
has poetic aspirations himself, he pulls the prisoner
away from the work detail to receive poetry lessons
from the celebrated Jewish writer. The bulk of the play
is their discussions of poetry, which the poet
is initially reluctant to have, the power differential
being so stark, and though he flatters the Kommandant
at first, when he begins to see his Nazi pupil's
true devotion to the art, as well as his untrained
and untapped talent, he goes to work in earnest,
and at times they are both simply lovers
of the German language, though the truth of their
situation often interrupts. In the last act,
the Kommandant is on trial for his crimes,
and in the days before he is to be executed,
he begs the poet to publish his work under his own name—
the Nazi's writing under the Jew's name—
because as a Nazi, he feels his own name is disgraced,
but he believes so strongly in poetry, that it matters
more to him that his work survive, than that anyone
know it was his work. The play is pulled entirely
from my imagination, a careful re-reading
of Simon Wiesenthal's *The Sunflower,* and the poetic ideas
of Rilke and Goethe with a smattering of Nietzsche.

In readings of the play, the Kommandant
has seemed more noble than I had intended—in many ways,
more noble than the Jew, because the Jew is suffering
by no fault of his own, while the Kommandant is tortured
by conscience, and driven by a sense of poetic calling
that separates him from the Germans around him.
On the morning of the third workshop reading, I watched
a video of two Russians on an ice dancing reality show
performing as Jews in Auschwitz. I was sickened,
even though I couldn't follow the pantomimed action,
and I wondered if I was producing Holocaust kitsch myself,
if my work was as disgusting as theirs, though I knew
if I asked any of my team, they would reassure me
that I am doing important work that rises to the level
of art. Last night, during a break in the workshop of the play,
I told the story of how my Grandmother, upon learning
that her entire family had died in the camps,
had burned the photo albums of everyone she had loved.
I have told that story many, many times,
without feeling much more than regret, or sympathy,
but this time I broke down crying, and I couldn't stop.
Everyone at the table came to comfort me,
and I felt ridiculous, but the only thing I could say was,
"It's time for us to go. This isn't a place we can live anymore."
I left the studio embarrassed, and later that day,
I resigned from the production. I don't think they believed

that I was serious, and they'll expect me to show up
at the next table reading. I won't. The play will go on
though I can have nothing more to do with it.
This morning, after taking a shirt off the hanger,
I looked in the mirror and realized I hadn't put it on.
Without thinking, I had started packing a bag.

December 2016

WOLVES I HAVE KNOWN (FOUND POEM)

All text taken from "Wolves I Have Known," by Marilyn Monroe as told to Florabel Muir
in the January 1953 issue of Motion Picture and Television Magazine

About 2 a.m. I heard someone prowling around the window.
I was scared silly. I got up and tiptoed around to the window

and I could see that a man was trying to cut the screen.
I said I thought he was a policeman. They found his badge

and identification in his pocket and he admitted he had met me
and thought he'd come call on me. They took him to jail,

and he doesn't wear a badge anymore. If you are born with sex
appeal, you can either let it wreck you or use it to your advantage.

He followed me upstairs when I went to get my wrap and trapped me . . .
I managed to get loose and ran into another room. Shut out, he pounded

on the door and pleaded that he just wanted to talk with me. I found
a magazine and sat quietly while he roared. After a while he left.

One of these characters telephoned me one night and said
he would be over in ten minutes. I didn't squeal with delight or anything.

The things a gal has to think up to outwit these predatory males!

BLOOD AND SOIL

Let me lift my shirt for you.

    Let me bear my throat.

One dollar! One dollar!

    Cut as deep as you like!

One dollar! The Bloodless Boy Wonder!

    Money back if he bleeds!

I have no blood. No soil.

    I have bones and muscle and skin.

But no land. No blood.

    Cut anywhere you want lady.

The boy sure hopes you're shy.

    The easiest customers

are the big men

    who want to figure out the trick.

There is no trick.

    Just me, and a knife,

and a tent, and a barker.

    I stay perfectly silent.

Their faces start red,

    but turn white

when nothing comes out

    as the blade goes in.

Some find God

    inside me.

I say, *Home is*

    where the knives are.

What Jew doesn't wander?

    When they come with their torches,

shouting *Blood and Soil*, I think

    If I had those, I'd be as poor

as you. I think

    That's just ordinary.

I think *Someone should blow out all*

    their big, stupid candles.

If all you want is dirt,

    it's everywhere you go.

Just look down

    at the dirt you walk on.

If all you want is blood,

    I can show you how easy

it is to cut. Most people

    can find all the blood

they ever wanted,

    right there inside themselves.

Right beneath the skin,

    where it's been hiding.

THE PARABLE OF THE DICTATOR

After the death of the dictator, his son wanted him embalmed. His son wanted him on perpetual display in a glass box.

No one knew what the dictator had wanted. The dictator had made it a crime to even speak of his death. He had not left instructions for his corpse.

The dictator's son summoned our country's most skilled embalmers and put them to work on embalming his father. He announced the project with great fanfare.

Shortly after, the dictator's daughter interrupted the embalmers, putting a stop to the project. She wanted to dictator's body be hollowed out for her to wear as a suit on special occasions.

The embalmers told her that a full body suit would not be possible. They explained that they were not taxidermists, but rather embalmers. She had the embalmers shot, and brought in taxidermists, along with a number of bear corpses for the taxidermists to use for practice.

When the dictator's son learned of his sister's interference, he had the taxidermists shot, and brought in new embalmers. The daughter, in turn, had the new embalmers shot and brought in new taxidermists.

The dictator's son laid a trap for his sister, but she fled the capital for the safety of one of her strongholds. Packing lightly, she took only the dictator's severed head, which had been fashioned into a mask for her to wear.

In the long civil war that followed, the daughter of the dictator regularly addressed her followers in long speeches while wearing her father's head. The faction led by the son of the dictator were particularly furious about the body of the dictator not being on display in a glass box.

As we watched the dictator's daughter's speech on the giant screen in our re-educational detention center, you reminded me that in the time before the dictator had become the dictator, I had admired his daughter's perfect teeth. Oddly, I was warmed by the memory. We still had a house then.

Before the dictator, it had been normal to think about having nice teeth or nice hair. In those days, we thought a lot about our happiness, and what to wear.

I made a joke about mindfulness and you laughed silently, so the guards wouldn't notice us talking or holding hands. Now, as I look up at the screen, I think, well this is happening. And it is.

STALINISM III (THE CLOUD ATLAS)

The "Atlas," which contains twenty-eight views, is now the official cloud atlas of the world, and the illustrations in it are the type to which all cloud forms must hereafter be referred.
—*The Photographic News*, 1896

We started a school against schools.

We made a rule against rules.

We shamed people for shaming people.

We singled people out for singling people out.

Our manifestos were read with care.

Our screeds were read with anger.

Our complaints were received with compliance.

We removed authors from the bookshelves.

We removed teachers from the classrooms.

We told outrageous lies.

We made monstrous allegations.

We were very successful.

Someone called us incoherent, so we went on the attack.

Someone called us abhorrent, so we petitioned for their removal.

So many eggs to break.

So many omelets, getting cold.

⁂

It only takes one lie in an honest man's mouth

to make him a liar.

It only takes one false accusation
to muddy the waters.
If you make people angry enough,
they'll do all your dirty work,
and you don't even have to ask.

❧

No one knew what to call us.
Or even exactly who we were.
I called us The Cloud Atlas,
because we had invented
nothing new. We only recognized
patterns that have existed
since the beginning of time.
Since the beginning of people.

❧

Do you know what's persuasive?
Repetition.
You just have to say it over and over
and people will be pretty sure
it must be true.

꘎

Do you want to know what we're doing right now?

It's whatever we'll accuse you of tomorrow.

You might have already been accused.

꘎

Do you know the story of how Stalin died?

His biographers tend to emphasize

that the doctors were too afraid

to treat him. That he might have lived

had he received swifter treatment.

But here's what I think is important:

He was at home, comfortable, safe.

His grip on power was secure.

His incompetence and cruelty rewarded

even to the moment he died.

What Stalin knew is what I know:

That the only way to die

in your own bed

is to make sure

no one else does.

STALINISM IV (FRIDA KAHLO)

In her very last painting, Frida Kahlo painted Joseph Stalin.
Joseph Stalin had assassinated her lover, Leon Trotsky, a Jew,
or rather in English: "Jew." Trotsky would have said "Иврей"
—*Eevray*—the ethnicity, not the religion, if you can parse the two;
I can't. I could, until I lived in Russia and was *eevray* myself,
the people around me seeing it in my face. Try explaining
(in halting Russian) that you can't *look Jewish* to people who think
you look *eevraysky* (and are right) and aren't asking because
they don't like you, but because they think you're one of them.
Try to tell them about Whoopi Goldberg and Scarlett Johansson
and Peggy Lipton and Rashida Jones. The Hebrew word
for Hebrew is עִבְרִית—*eevreet*—cousin of *eevray,* cousin of *Hebrew.*
Lev Bronstein, like my Grandmother, was born in the Pale
of Settlement, an area created in 1791 by Catherine the Great
to contain the Jewish population of her recently conquered lands.
Lev Bronstein became Leon Trotsky because it was the name
in the false passport he used to escape Czarist Russia. The name
stuck. Ioseb Jughashvili, who took the name Joseph Stalin
(Stalin meaning "Man of Steel"), would refer to Trotsky
as *Bronstein* as a kind of slur, mirrored in English where "Jew"
has the odd distinction of being the only name for a group
of people that is the proper name and an offensive term
at the same time. Stalin hated Jews. He purged Jews
from the upper ranks of Soviet society. He had thirteen
of the Soviet Union's most prominent Yiddish language writers
murdered in a single night. My grandmother called Yiddish

"Jewish" because "Yid" is the Yiddish word for "Jew."
Diego Rivera considered himself Jewish, as he was descended
from *conversos*, Jews who had decided to convert
to avoid the Inquisition, and while Frida Kahlo's father
was not actually Jewish, she seems to have believed he was,
and despite Judaism being matrilineal, she spoke of herself
as Jewish. When Rivera and Kahlo checked into a "restricted"
hotel in Detroit, she declared herself Jewish, and as they
were guests of Henry Ford, the hotel changed their policy
to admit Jews, the irony here being that Henry Ford
hated Jews, going as far to publish books like *The International Jew:
The World's Foremost Problem.* Ford even received The Grand Cross
of the German Eagle, the highest award that Nazi Germany
bestowed on foreigners. It doesn't surprise me that Kahlo said
she was Jewish when she was not. It doesn't surprise me
that Kahlo took Trotsky to her bed and then painted
his executioner. During the Second World War, when the generals
of the Red Army asked Stalin to outlaw rape, he encouraged it
instead, and outlawed being captured as a prisoner of war.
In 1945, at the behest of the Soviet Ambassador to Mexico,
Frida Kahlo sent a large scale work—more than six feet wide—
to the Soviet Union as a gift of friendship. "La Mesa Herida,"
or "The Wounded Table." The Ambassador died in a plane crash
shortly after. By the time the work arrived in the Soviet Union,
the work was declared decadent and imperialist.
Surrealism had become an affront to Soviet ideology, and

Kahlo's work was seen as surrealist. Kahlo had begun
"The Wounded Table" while divorcing Diego Rivera
over his affair with her sister, Cristina, though the rift
was short lived, and Rivera and Kahlo remarried within a year.
A committed Marxist, Kahlo found Rivera's difficult relationship
with organized communism to be quite painful. Rivera was expelled
from the Soviet Union in 1927, and resigned or was expelled
from the Mexican Communist Party many times. Hosting Trotsky
had made them suspect, and her late painting of Stalin
may have been a way to make clear her devotion to Communism.
What did Kahlo know when she painted Stalin? Did she know
of the Doctor's Plot? Of the murdered poets? Of the terrors?
Of the starved Kolkhozes? Of the show trials? Of sanctioned rape?
Of the thirteen-year-old orphan Stalin impregnated in his thirties?
On my desk is a little box with a decoupaged self portrait
of Frida Kahlo, a gift from my best friend, with whom I studied
Kahlo's work in college, and If I were a different sort of person,
I'd take it off my desk, in protest. But I love my friend.
I love Kahlo's face. While I'm lost in thought, looking
at this little box, a student asks me, shaking me from my train
of thought, "What happened to Guns N' Roses?" and I tell her
that if I recall correctly, they recorded a Charles Manson song,
without telling their record label, and even though we didn't
call it that then, they were cancelled. I think there's more
but Wikipedia confirms the basic outlines of the story.
My student asks, "Why are people attracted to evil?" which is

a stunningly good question, and I respond (surprising myself), "Because it's freeing." We talk about Eldridge Cleaver and Bill Cosby, about the Marquis de Sade, Caligula, Roy Cohn. We talk about Frida Kahlo painting Stalin.

CLICK BAIT

Today's distraction: an article on how to avoid distraction.

Turn off notifications. Clear your desktop. Divide things

into what you are working on now and what you will

work on later. Schedule the day. Use a timer. Reward yourself

when you finish a task. Spoiler alert: It won't work.

Remember the "French wardrobe" in which you only owned

variations of one outfit to avoid "decision fatigue"?

(See also, ordering the first thing on any menu; see also,

ordering the same meal at every restaurant.) Question:

is writing this poem a form of distraction or a form of focus?

Am I trying to avoid something more pressing by writing

this poem? Or is this my life's work, and the only thing

that truly matters? Yesterday's distraction: an article

about "toxic productivity" and the value of sloth.

I like the word "toxic," and how now you can put it in front

of anything. Toxic positivity. Toxic masculinity. Toxic futurity.

What if after this poem, we take a break? I'll stop writing

and you'll close this book, not for too long, ten minutes,

say. Twenty if you need more time. We can set a timer.

We can turn off our notifications. It can be our

asynchronous secret, something we did together

though we've never even met. Something that brought

us calm in a world that everyone agrees is spinning too fast.

We'll make a little island, where my only distraction is you.

BLOOD LIBEL / MY THROTE IS KUT

"My throte is kut unto my nekke boon,"
Seyde this child, "and as by wey of kynde
I sholde have dyed, ye, longe tyme agon."
—Chaucer, *The Prioress's Tale*, 1399

Drynke ye alle herof; this is my blood of the newe testament,
which schal be sched for many, in to remissioun of synnes
—Matthew 26:28, *The Wycliffe Bible*, 1395

For roughly three years in our brand new century,
at a business called Ambrosia (the food of the gods
or a marshmallow salad depending on whom you ask),
older people feeling sluggish could be infused
with the blood of younger people, for the low, low price
of eight thousand dollars a liter. There was one center
in Florida, one in California, and as you might expect,
one more to open in New York, before the FDA
shut them down. Shortly after the first syringe was invented,
in 1659, the first blood transfusion took place, the blood
of a healthy lamb injected into the circulatory system
of a man with a fever, and after that went well,
more lamb blood was injected into more humans,
until some of those humans began dying, and a widow
sued for her husband's death, leading to the outlawing
of the practice, at least in France, at least until
the early 1900s, when the discovery of blood types
allowed for blood transfusions between humans to be safely
carried out. Everyone I know is obsessed with blood,

metaphorically speaking, with ancestry, with what
has been passed down, getting DNA tests to tell them
where their genetic ancestors had lived in the 1300s,
and I am twice traitor to my blood, an adoptee taking
residence in a community to which I have no "blood ties"
and a childless man, letting my bloodline stop with me,
the decadent hero of my own little novel, cultivating art
at the future's expense. In Kafka stories, the young protagonist
often dies or withers just as his father finds new vitality,
and I think too much about Gregor Samsa's blood,
and what it turns into when he becomes *ungeziefer*,
typically translated as "vermin," though commonly understood
as "bug." Kafka died in 1924, sparing him the horrors
of the Holocaust, though *Terezin* was in his home town
of Prague, the model concentration camp pulled straight
from his stories, shown to the Red Cross by the Nazis
to prove their humanity, when they too were obsessed
with blood, shouting slogans, like "Blood and Soil."
Kafka's blood was Jewish, like mine, or not like mine,
who knows, though sometimes I imagine the famously wan
and depressed young Kafka donating his blood
to some aging tech billionaire, which in my imagined story,
makes the tech billionaire lethargic and despondent,
unable to do much beyond see the inherent absurdity
in his fortune, in his tech, in his life. If I were a novelist,
I'd know what happens next, but I'm a poet, so that's

as far as I can see. At Harvard, young mice and old mice
are having their bloodstreams linked for study.
It's called *parabiosis*, and while the research looks promising
for the old mice, no one seems too concerned about
the young mice, as long as they don't die. Jews are forbidden
the consumption of blood, required to drain the carcasses
they plan to eat, to salt the meat, to draw out the blood.
Jews are forbidden to eat any part of a living animal.
In Eastern Europe, the Jews we met used only clear alcohol
for kiddush: schnapps or vodka, avoiding wine, to avoid
the accusation of using blood in their rituals, an accusation
that seems to have originated in twelfth century England,
but has been surprisingly durable, spreading outward,
morphing, surviving many ages of reason, and surfacing
most recently as "Frazzeldrip," a conspiracy theory
in which drinking blood and mutilating children is standard
left wing practice, which is why it has become standard
right wing practice to show up with guns where these children
are believed to be. In *The Canterbury Tales*, "The Prioress's Tale"
recounts a child being ritualistically murdered by Jews,
but when the Jews throw the boy's body into the privy,
his corpse sings a hymn that allows his body to be found.
My throat is cut down to the neck bone, said this child,
and by way of man, I should have died. I shouldn't be surprised
anymore, that people believe such outlandish stories,
especially when those stories are covered with blood.

I get so angry that I live in an age of unreason, but all ages
are ages of unreason. I get so angry when I think of how little
we are doing to escape the danger we all know we're in.
Below my screen, I see my aging hands, the skin beginning
to show the tendons and blood vessels that move as I type.
The Red Cross stopped taking my blood the very first time
I made love to a man, and I'm much too old for anyone
in Silicon Valley to pay for my blood anymore,
which is to say that no one wants my blood now
unless maybe poetry itself is a kind of a parabiosis.
Maybe I've already begun bleeding into you, and you
are metabolizing me now, my blood in your blood,
my flesh in your flesh. There is a painting from the
Spanish inquisition that depicts a family of Jews
torturing the wafer, Christ's body, in private,
and a trickle of blood flows from the wafer, so slight the Jews
don't see that it has run a thread thin river out the door,
alerting the inquisitors to come and put the Jewish family
to death. What is it Christ says? The Christ
I am said to have killed? The Christ I don't believe in?
Drink you all hereof; this is my blood of the new testament,
which shall be shed for many, into remission of sins.
I am no Christ. I am no martyr. My blood is not magic
or redemptive or salvific. My blood is my blood, and yes,
of course, my blood does sing, though not to call out
for violence or revenge. The human heart knows just one tune,

an iambic thumping in time to the breath, the restless blood
traversing our bodies at incredible speed, and if you put
your ear to my chest, you will feel the gentle pulsing
of my beating heart, and you will hear the only song
my heart can sing, because inside us all, is a beautiful noise,
a beautiful human noise.

SUMMER

I was on the beach, it was morning, it was summer,
the gay men sparsely dotting the sand in their skimpy
bathing suits, and I realized I was in the opening scene
of *Longtime Companion,* that here I was firmly
in the before of every movie that had ever offered to tell
the story of my peoples: the happy Jews in 1930s
Europe riding their bicycles among the trees;
the dancing men in the 1970s, blissful in the dark.
I saw in that moment that I was at the end
of an idyll, that as the world is always ending
for someone, now it would be ending for me.
And then there was the shooing. And then the flags
were at half mast, and it made no difference:
the preparation, the rainbows, the grief.

June 12, 2016.

III

GAY DIVORCE (FREE RADICAL)

I'm a free radical. An unpaired sock. My axis
of symmetry is broken. I'm the sum of one part,
a cup with no saucer, a hand with no ring,
a book with no sequel, a phone with no charger.
I am my own square root. You can raise me
to any power, and just end up with me.
I thought I was a balloon. I thought I was a kite.
I thought I could fly as high as I wanted,
and that you would always be there on the ground,
holding my string, reeling me in when it was time
to go home. Now I'm a loosed kite. A balloon let go.
I was always afraid of heights, until I believed
that no matter how far I fell, you would be there
to catch me. When did you stop wanting
to catch me? When did I stop wanting to be caught?
I am whole, but I am halved. I am one left shoe,
on my own two feet. I am making brand new tracks
in the newly fallen snow.

GAY DIVORCE (10TH AVENUE)

These streets are so bright now, in what was once the gloom of Manhattan's
outer edge, the giant glowing logos beaming their fluorescent success stories
into what I remember as a place of loading and unloading, of cheap real estate,
of too much exhaust. Well done, Tenth Avenue. Well done, Whole Foods.
Well done, Peloton. Well done, H&M. I'm only two drinks in, perhaps three,
(four if you count that double as two), treading my way home from a daytime
dance party, a lunch, a friend, his friends, a leather bar, and it's early enough
that the trains are still only five minutes apart, and home I go to my clean sheets
and empty bed, empty but for me, empty but for my one pillow. I love
New York for the way it makes you feel small but welcomed. Always in these
streets, I feel both insignificant and special. New York is always saying,
Would you like some cheap pizza? Did you see this architectural marvel?
Did that rat scare you? If I'd stayed a little longer at the bar I could
have woken up in a stranger's bed, which I'm allowed to do now, no check in,
no betrayal, no repercussion, but I'm afraid of those beds now, remembering
how I used to use them to sample the lives I might live, until I woke up
in one that I never left. Until now. But still. It's too risky. I don't have another
twenty years to spend with another stranger. At the leather bar, my friend
was asking his friend about disco, specifically about the music released
between 1978 and 1982, which seemed a bit narrow to me, but I listened
with curiosity and when the conversation turned to black lights and body paint,
I mentioned the famous photograph of Bill T. Jones, his body painted
by Keith Haring, covered in those famous squiggly lines, documented by
Tseng Kwong Chi, but even that's not quite right. They were collaborators.
The piece belonged to all of them, but that's not how it got remembered.
No one seemed to know what I was talking about, so I Googled it and everyone

recognized it instantly. The disco expert pointed out the painted stripes
on Jones's cock, which I took to mean that he was distracted by his sex,
or rather that, like most people, he cannot reconcile the erotic with the aesthetic,
even though the two have never been better joined than in disco music,
which is supposedly his area of expertise. Then I thanked everyone,
took my leave, walked into the dark night, alone in the evening gloom
punctuated by bright logos and cheap pizza. I want to tell everyone
that my marriage is over. I want New York to make it all better. But that's
hardly New York's style. Or mine. At the pizza place, I ask for a slice of plain,
rather than explain that I haven't been alone this way in twenty-one years.
In the brand new train station, I ask a woman which stairs will take me
to the train I need, rather than explain that we didn't grow apart as much
as we learned the ways in which we were incompatible. The truth is that
New York is a teacher with only one lesson: How to be sad. How to live
with sadness. Tenth Avenue wants to know if I'd like to look in a window,
if I'd like to cross the street, if I'd like to be illuminated by a glowing sign.
The train station wants to know if I like its modern design and open spaces.
The subway wants to know if the molded plastic was good for sitting on.
My pillow wants to know if its soft enough, and if I'll be sleeping on my side
or my back tonight. New York wraps me in its endlessly interrupted darkness,
which is not the same as trying to cheer me up. I may finally have learned
my lesson.

GAY DIVORCE
(QUEEN-SIZED BED)

It seems obvious
that when sleeping alone
in a queen-sized bed,
the pillow should be moved
to the middle,
that I should
sleep in the middle.
The other pillow
can go on the floor
until morning.
But that's habit for you.
Sleeping on one side
of the bed as though
the other side still
belonged to you.
If you would like this
to be a metaphor,
I won't mind.
Here I am, figuring out how
to take up all the space
I used to share.
Here I am
replacing your warmth
with an extra blanket.

THE UNTREATED BURN

It hurt when I touched the oven rack
while adjusting the roast,
but I underestimated the burn,
didn't stop to ice it,
just continued with the ache,
finished preparing the meal,
serving the dinner,
eating the food,
cleaning up after.
I forgot the burn
until the days following
when my finger began
to blister and swell,
the fourth finger
on my right hand
unable to bend,
a reminder that wounds
get worse
when they go untreated.

FROM *A PILLOW BOOK*

after Sei Shōnagon

80. Things that have lost their power.

> A red speedo on a man who, though once quite rigorous about playing sport and lifting weights, has not been active in many years.
>
> A long, delicate cigarette holder, carved from ivory, and destined for the lips of a femme fatale in an age where smoking conjures images of throat tubes and brown teeth.
>
> Macrame after 1980.

81. Awkward things.

> A man greets another man, and although the second man doesn't remember the first man, he says nothing when the first man says, "I thought that was you!" They chat for five or ten minutes, as the second man becomes more and more sure that they do not in fact know each other. As they talk, the first man realizes that the second man is not at all who he thought he was. They shake hands and promise to keep in better touch. They are relieved at parting.
>
> An ankle-length cape, worn as part of an elaborate costume to an extravagant costume party, but that trips its wearer on the steps of the subway.
>
> When a cab driver cannot quite hear the passenger and drives to the right address, but in Manhattan, not Brooklyn.

74. Things that lose by being painted.

> Exposed brick.
>
> Coffee filters.
>
> Computer screens.
>
> Trees.

75. Things that gain by being painted.

       Furniture made of particle board.

       Painted brick.

       Drag queens.

       Blank canvases.

78. Things that give a hot feeling.

       When on the subway, a particularly beautiful man boards the train
           wearing a tank top and sits next to you, and his scent is light, but
           unavoidably there.

       A Facebook status update in which someone obliquely, obscurely,
           and inaccurately references something you did, and fifty people
           immediately comment to condemn you without knowing that you are
           the one being condemned.

YOU DO NOT HAVE AN INNER CHILD

The Education majors joke that all teachers gravitate
toward students who are the same age as their inner child,
except it's not a joke, they really believe it, the way
my friend who uses psychedelics and spirit guides to talk
to her two-year-old self, believes in her inner child.
The problem with inner children is that it treats childhood
as a kind of primer, the coat of paint that goes on the wall
first, the coat you have to get right, no drips, full coverage,
because otherwise the next layers of paint will never be right,
will peel, will flake, but here's the thing: people aren't walls.
You can't sand off the topcoat and regress. Children
are not tiny adults, and they can't comprehend things
adults can. There are no inner children because children
are not tree trunks, accumulating additional outer layers,
and they are not seeds, containing some future you.
They are saplings, little beings with their very own
needs and lives, and they are not inner or outer. I have
the pictures my parents made me stay in and draw
when I was too hysterical to leave the house, prone
to tantrums and meltdowns, and I'm not sure anyone
believes my story about the time I was five and stood
on top of my desk at school screaming that I wasn't bad
until my mother had to come in and carry me away
because I wouldn't let anyone else get close enough
to me to get me off the desk. All the pictures I drew
were of people crying, long-legged people crying,

short-legged people crying, and some of the explanations
are in my handwriting and some are in my mother's.
It's not that the person who drew those pictures isn't me,
it's that he's not the first coat of paint you can sand me
away to find. The only things inside me are blood
and muscle and bone and tendon. It's that he's not
in some suspended animation waiting for me to come
give him some love so he can heal. I keep trying
to explain the history of childhood to the Education
majors, to explain that their notion of childhood
comes from Wordsworth, that the Romantic movement
shifted understandings of what childhood means, but they
don't care. They tell me that people used to be wrong,
but now they know, and now they're right. They tell
me what actual children are like, while also telling me
about the actual children they keep nested deep inside.
Even if I told them what had happened to me, they
wouldn't understand. They'd think I'm telling them
about someone else, about some little boy that lives on
inside me like some nesting doll, but that little boy
isn't somewhere else. He's not a separate person.
He's not an artifact, or a fly in amber. There's just me.
I'm here. I'm here with everything I remember.
I'm right here.

WOUNDED, NOT BROKEN

I think you were the one who told me
that the defining feature of alcoholics
is that they experience all their emotions
as anger, that shame becomes anger, love
becomes anger, sadness becomes anger,
grief becomes anger, and so on and so on,
and I thought about how sad that was, but
also I saw the appeal in making everything
anger, the way you would never have to be
scared or lonely or ashamed, but in those days
I thought that anger was something that
left the body, that anger was a projectile
you aimed at another person, and not a furnace
that burns a person from the inside.
Grief is the hardest emotion to live with,
because you hold it all yourself, because
whatever you lost is lost, and if alcohol
is the alchemy that lets the dull gravity
of grief turn to the hot fire of rage, I get that.
Sometimes I wonder why I spend
so much time thinking about feelings,
though I don't think it's strange I spend
so much time thinking about language
or thinking about bodies. My biggest fear
is that I'm broken, that something is so wrong
with me that I can never be fixed,

and that I'll spend my whole life
trying to repair myself and never
managing it. But if I say I'm wounded,
not broken, that feels better.
If I'm wounded, I might still heal.

DESIRE

I don't want a new phone.

Or a new boy band.

But thank you,

for the offer.

It's a very nice phone.

A very nice boy band.

I never thought phones

would be the kind of thing

I thought about very much,

or spent a lot of money acquiring.

And I somehow thought

that boy bands would age

out of existence,

without replicating

themselves in ever younger

younger men.

I thought boy bands

were like Lawrence Welk,

or telegrams. Period pieces

to run their course

and then be discontinued.

But no. They keep coming

in unstable molecules

of boys, brought together

by the covalent bonds of

managers, youth,

desire, and money,

and they keep

spinning off

into solo careers

like so much smooth-bodied

dandelion fluff,

carried on the celebrity

winds of media.

Please don't think I'm saying

that I've had enough

of phone calls

or harmonies.

I will want both

as long as I'm alive.

You could call me right now.

I'd love to hear your voice.

I just don't need

a new phone.

I just don't need

a new boy band.

I've fallen in love

enough times

in my life.

FORTY-TWO

(in memory of Stanley Plumly, 1939–2019)

Somehow related to having entered my fifth decade of life,
childhood memories have started flooding back at odd moments.
Yesterday, I suddenly remembered a blue wall with white clouds
that a bunch of us kids were painting white so that the clouds
were just wall colored, or perhaps so the wall became cloud colored.
I felt the weight of the roller in my small hand, remembered
the feeling of the paint as it squished its whiteness over the blue.
I remembered a packet of novelty matches at a gift store in London,
the aisles of the store filled with toys and souvenirs, one plastic match
springing out like a penis, a glimpse of the pornographic that was
mostly hidden in the nineteen-seventies. The memories come unbidden,
little glimpses of a larger scene as I turn a corner, a tactile sensation
long gone as I try on clothes or start making lunch, relics of a past
so far gone as to be alien or unavailable, though some of the shames
still sting, and some triumphs return with a shock of pleasure.
Stan died yesterday, so it's no surprise he's been coming back to me
all day, memories of his office door with conference sign-up sheets
or the way he sat at my thesis defense, or the way I would work
myself into a hysteria about whatever poem I was about to show him,
my fears that it would be insulting or obscene, and how he
would calm me down, every time, unshockable by anything my still
adolescent self considered a terrible violation of decorum. The last time
he saw me, and this was recently, not decades ago, he said,
"You done good, kid," and someone might point out that I said
"the last time he saw me" and not "the last time I saw him" as though
I'm telling you a story about him and not a story about me, as though

I live my life as though I were not the person at the center of it.

The past used to come up only when it made sense, like the time

I apologized to a doctor for my very small veins, just before a hernia exam,

and the doctor smiled at me with the kindly puzzlement I love him for,

and said, "I'm not feeling for your veins," at which point

I did remember the doctor who told me I had very small veins during

a hernia exam, when I was fourteen, and how he apologized for spending

so much time with his fingers in my scrotum, and how I slowly became

erect, embarrassed at my lack of self-control, and hoping that

the mandatory second adult in the room wouldn't tell the other

Boy Scouts that I'd gotten hard during the exam, but now it seems

more likely that this doctor wasn't going to let go of my testicles

until he saw me hard, and I wonder why he lied, and if all the Boy Scouts

of Troop Four-Forty-Seven share the same secret, or if he was

especially curious about my penis, and who that second adult

would have told had he thought that this doctor, father of one of the other boys,

was giving hernia exams that seemed to result in a surprisingly high rate

of erections, unless it was just me, and I wonder why that doctor

lied about veins like that, a stupid lie, one easily caught, even though

I didn't catch it until decades later, in the form of my apologizing

for something that was never even really wrong with my body.

My mother warned me that when I had children, all of my traumas

would come back to me one by one, as I watched my children

live through the ages of whatever had hurt me, but I never had children,

so maybe that's why these memories are coming back now, in a giant jumble

of unrelated scenes and glimpses, like the white clouds on a blue wall,

or the way I would go through the hotel with the maids and leave
orange sodas in the fridge, and chocolates on the pillows, back when
orange sodas and pillow chocolates were the most indulgent treats
I could imagine the world had to offer. Stan would tell me stories
about his life, and I loved them in a way I was too embarrassed
to tell him. I loved the stories about his refusing to sign a loyalty oath
and losing his art scholarship, and the stories about the not quite
step-son giving Stan's girlfriend so much trouble. I thought
that I would never have such important stories, and the truth is
that I don't. I've never made sense of my life. I've never had a clear
story, where I'm the hero at the center. What comes back to me
is disconnected and irrelevant, anecdotal and sensory, a wall,
a matchbook, a foot massage, a hernia exam, the feeling of the ceiling
against my back when I was being punished. I miss you, Stan,
the way you were never shocked, the way you never aged,
except to let your beard grow steadily whiter, how you seemed
to know exactly who you were and what you thought was right,
and how even if it wasn't true, you looked so solidly at the center
of your own life, a kind of sun, holding everything around you
in place with your gravity, and how I was sure that would never
quite happen to me, how I feared I'd never fully make sense,
even to myself, but how it reassured me, that as long as someone
knew how to live, it would be OK if I never quite figured it out.

BIOGRAPHICAL NOTE

Jason Schneiderman is the author of five poetry collections and the editor of the anthology *Queer: A Reader for Writers* (Oxford UP 2016). His poems and essays have appeared in numerous journals and anthologies. His awards include the Emily Dickinson Award, the Shestack Award, and a Fulbright Fellowship. He is a longtime cohost of the podcast *Painted Bride Quarterly Slush Pile* and has guest hosted American Public Media's *The Slowdown*. He is a professor of English at the Borough of Manhattan Community College and teaches in the MFA Program for Writers at Warren Wilson. He lives in New York City.